First World War
and Army of Occupation
War Diary
France, Belgium and Germany

14 DIVISION
43 Infantry Brigade,
Brigade Trench Mortar Battery
5 July 1918 - 30 September 1918

WO95/1910/7

The Naval & Military Press Ltd
www.nmarchive.com
Published in association with The National Archives

Published by

The Naval & Military Press Ltd

Unit 10 Ridgewood Industrial Park,

Uckfield, East Sussex,

TN22 5QE England

Tel: +44 (0) 1825 749494

www.naval-military-press.com

www.nmarchive.com

This diary has been reprinted in facsimile from the original. Any imperfections are inevitably reproduced and the quality may fall short of modern type and cartographic standards.

© Crown Copyright
Images reproduced by permission of The National Archives, London, England, 2015.

Contents

Document type	Place/Title	Date From	Date To
Heading	WO95/1910/6a. 14 Div-43 Inf Bde Bde T M Batty Jul-Sep 1918		
Heading	14th Division 43rd Infy Bde 43rd Trench Mortar Bty Jly 1918-Sep 1918		
Miscellaneous	To A.G. Bare	02/08/1918	02/08/1918
War Diary	Boulogne	05/07/1918	05/07/1918
War Diary	Boursin	06/07/1918	11/07/1918
War Diary	Licques	11/07/1918	12/07/1918
War Diary	Tournehem	12/07/1918	13/07/1918
War Diary	Bayenghem	13/07/1918	18/07/1918
War Diary	Quesques	19/07/1918	31/07/1918
Miscellaneous	43rd Trench Mortar Battery Programme of Training for week ending July 13th 1918	13/07/1918	13/07/1918
Miscellaneous	43 Trench Mortar Battery Programme of Training for 3 days ending July 17th 1918	17/07/1918	17/07/1918
Miscellaneous	French Mortar Course-Battery Commencing 18th July dispensing 1st Augt	18/07/1918	18/07/1918
War Diary	Quesques	01/08/1918	01/08/1918
War Diary	Ouest Mont	01/08/1918	13/08/1918
War Diary	Lederzeele	13/08/1918	14/08/1918
War Diary	Bissezeele	14/08/1918	15/08/1918
War Diary	Droglandt	15/08/1918	17/08/1918
War Diary	Proven	17/08/1918	18/08/1918
War Diary	A. 30 Central	18/08/1918	19/08/1918
War Diary	Ypres Front	19/08/1918	31/08/1918
Miscellaneous	43rd Trench Mortar Battery Training Programme for Week ending August 10th 1918	10/08/1918	10/08/1918
Miscellaneous	14th Division. Ref Map 27A. S.E.	06/08/1918	06/08/1918
Operation(al) Order(s)	43rd Trench Mortar Battery Operation Order No.1.	18/08/1918	18/08/1918
Operation(al) Order(s)	43rd Trench Mortar Battery Operation Order No. 2.	23/08/1918	23/08/1918
Operation(al) Order(s)	43rd Trench Mortar Battery Operation Order No. 3	30/08/1918	30/08/1918
Operation(al) Order(s)	43rd Trench Mortar Battery Operation Order No. 4	01/09/1918	01/09/1918
War Diary	Ypres Front. Ref Map (28. N.W.4)	01/09/1918	11/09/1918
War Diary	Ypres Front	11/09/1918	14/09/1918
War Diary	School Camp Ref Map. 27. L.3.C.5.5.	15/09/1918	20/09/1918
War Diary	Dominion Camp Sheet. 28. C.23.b.8.6.	21/09/1918	23/09/1918
War Diary	G.26b. 2a99	24/09/1918	27/09/1918
War Diary	Line. Ref Maps 28. N.W.4. 28 S.W.2	27/09/1918	28/09/1918
War Diary	G.21. b.90.99 Ref Map Belgium 1/20000	29/09/1918	30/09/1918
Operation(al) Order(s)	Operation Order No. 6. Reference Map: Sheet 28 N.W. 1/20,000 & Sheet 27 1/40,000	14/09/1918	14/09/1918
Operation(al) Order(s)	43rd Trench Mortar Battery Operation Order No. 5 Reference Map Ypres 1/10000 28 1/40000	11/09/1918	11/09/1918
Miscellaneous	C Form. Messages And Signals.		
Heading	Nomu ASH Nomu for his report aplise		
Miscellaneous	43rd Trench Mortar Battery Move Order Reference Map. 28 1/20,000	20/09/1918	20/09/1918

No. 85/1910 — 6d

14 Div — 43 Inf Bde

Bde T M Batty

Jul–Sep 1918

14TH DIVISION
43RD INFY BDE

43RD TRENCH MORTAR BTY
JLY 1918-SEP 1918

14TH DIVISION
43RD INFY BDE

To
A.G.   4
  Base.

43RD
TRENCH MORTAR
BATTERY.

No. A 29
2/8/18

Herewith War Diary
for month of July

[signature] Capt.
Comdg. 43° T.M.B.

WAR DIARY or INTELLIGENCE SUMMARY

Army Form C. 2118

43 TM By
July '18 – Sep '18

Place	Date	Hour	Summary of Events and Information	Remarks and references to Appendices
BOULOGNE	5-7-18	11.40	The 43rd Light Trench Mortar Battery unded the command of Capt. S.R.F. HIDE MC arrived at BOULOGNE from FOLKESTONE to join the B.E.F. Strength 4 Officers (2/Lt. G.A. HICKS. 4ESSEX. REGT. 2/Lt. T.W. DAVIS. BEDFORD REGT. 2/Lt. R. HARBISON (S.R.H.L.I.) and 51 O.R.	
BOURSIN	6-7-18	6.00	On arriving Battery proceeded to OSTROHOVE Rest camp. Weather fine	
			Battery left Rest camp entraining at BOULOGNE for MARQUISE Ry.	
		9.30	arr. CALAIS 13. todoo 3.C. 40.75. Arrived MARQUISE B.36. Ry.	
BOURSIN	7-7-18		Regiment CALAIS 13. todoo 3.E. 01.35 arrived 12.30. Weather fine	
BOURSIN	8-7-18		ORGANISATION + INTERIOR ECONOMY of Battery proceeded with. Weather fine	Programme attached
	9-7-18		Training on new training programme. Weather fine	
	10-7-18		Training on new training programme. Weather fine. Sundry at times. Wind. S'ly	
BOURSIN LICQUES	11-7-18	8.30 and 12.00	Training as per training programme. Weather Showery. Wind S. Battery "left" Boursin (43rd Inf Bde Order No 13) Arrived LICQUES (Ry hq. CALAIS 100 000 F.3 20 42) 12.00 HQrs Hotel de 2 Vielle Tournee Weather good	attached attached
LICQUES TOURNEHEM	12-7-18	9 pm 2 am	Battery left LICQUES (43rd Inf Bde Order 13). Arrived TOURNEHEM (Ref map A.3.) HAZEBROUCK 5A todoo) 12.000 H.Qrs Bielet 2.N. Weather very showery. Fair	attached
TOURNEHEM	13-7-18	8 pm	Battery left TOURNEHEM (43 Inf Bde Order 13/2) Arrived BAYENGHEM 10.10	
BAYENGHEM		10.10	Ry map HAZEBROUCK. 5A todoo B.3.45.65) MQrs Bt C.R. 37 Weather improved	attached

2449 Wt. W14957/M90 750,000 1/16 J.B.C. & A. Forms/C.2118/12.

Army Form C. 2118.

WAR DIARY
or
INTELLIGENCE SUMMARY
(Erase heading not required.)

Place	Date	Hour	Summary of Events and Information	Remarks and references to Appendices
BAYENGHEM	14-7-18	8.30	Church Parade. Weather showery. Divisional trumpets. 1 OR admitted to hospital.	gas hospital
	15-7-18		Training as programme. Weather unsettled.	
	16-7-18		Training as programme. Weather improves.	
	17-7-18		Brigade inspection by 2d Army Commander. Brigade interior.	
	18-7-18	9.30	Battery proceeds by lorries to XV Corps Weather unsettled. At Wather School at	
QUESQUES			QUESQUES (refused GRIS. 13. F.4. 30.42.) Arrived XV Corps above mentioned from	
QUESQUES	19-7-18	11.30	Commencement of courses in accordance with XV Corps school details.	
	20			
	21			
	22			
	23			
	24			
	25			
	26			
	27			
	28			
	29			
	30			
	31		1 OR hours to VK 1st class officers leave.	

43rd Trench Mortar Battery

Programme of Training for week ending July 13th 1918

Day of Week	8.30 - 9.30	9.30 - 10.30	10.45 - 11.45	11.45 - 12.45	2.15 - 2.45
Monday	Physical Training and Bayonet fighting	Infantry Training Sec. 47-74	Route March	Gun Drill	Cleaning Guns
Tuesday	Route March	Musketry and B.R. Drill	Physical Training and Bayonet fighting	Gun Drill	Cleaning Guns
Wednesday	Physical Training and Bayonet fighting	Infantry Training	Route March	Gun Drill	Lecture Chronicle
Thursday	← Firing →				
Friday	Physical Training and Bayonet fighting	Musketry	Route March	Gun Drill	Lecture Shells & Fuses
Saturday	← Firing →				Capt

Comdg. 43rd T.M. Bty

No 3 Trench Mortar Battery

Programme of Training for 3 days entraining 17th 1918

Day of Week	8.30 – 9.30	9.30 – 10.30	10.45 – 11.45	11.45 – 12.30	2.00 – 3.00	3.00 – 3.30
Monday	Physical Training and Bayonet fighting	Musketry	Route March	Gun Drill	Gun Drill	Enemy Guns
Tuesday	Carpentry Training	Musketry	Gun Drill	Route March Gun Drill	Gun Drill	
Wednesday	Route March	Carpentry Training	Physical Training and Bayonet fighting	Gun Drill	Gun Drill	

	Trench Mortar Course - Battery Commencing 18th July dispersing 1st Augt
Thurs 18	Assemble
Fri 19	M. Commandant's Address - Close Order drill A. General Description. Gun Drill
Sat 20	M. General Description (Cont'd) - Gun Drill
Mon 22	M. Care of Mortar & Ammunition - Miss fires, Blinds & Prematures - Gun Drill A. Digging recesses and Gun laying
Tues 23	M. Laying and Lines of Fire. Gun drill and digging recesses A. Dummy firing
Wed 24	M. Officers & N.C.O's. Ranging & Range Tables O.R. Battery Close Order Drill - Gun laying and Digging
Thurs 25	M. Half - Dummy Firing - Ranging & Registering Half - Gun Drill and Recapitulation A. Ditto
Fri 26	M. Tactical Handling of Light Mortars - Gun Drill A. Emplacements - Firing with Handles & Slings

Sat 27	M.	Anti Aircraft Work - Gun Drill - Preparing Ammunition & Guns.
Mon 29	M. Half. Half.	Live Firing Recapitulation
Tues 30	M. A.	Close Order Drill - Attack Formations, Coming into action Gun Drill & Competitions
Wed 31	M.	Reliefs and Routine - Present and Future Developments
Thurs 1.		Disperse

R. H. Hutchings Capt.
Chief Instructor T. M. 43 School

Army Form C. 2118.

43 L T M Bty
attach to Bn

WAR DIARY or INTELLIGENCE SUMMARY

(Erase heading not required.)

Place	Date	Hour	Summary of Events and Information	Remarks and references to Appendices
QUESQUES.	1-8-18	10am	Battery left Esquerdes school by Lorry.	
OUEST MONT		15.00	Ouest Mont (referred 27A N.E. Serno K.27.A) reached along road way N. from K.27.A. 85.15 (referred 27A N.E. Serno) Weather	
OUEST MONT	2-9-18		very fine. Training (P.T. & B.F. INFANTRY TRAINING. MUSKETRY & GUN DRILL) Weather	
	3-8-18		Training. Bathing. Organised games in afternoon. Weather very	
	4-8-18	9.00	Afternoon Sunday. Church Parade. Officers & N.C.O's attended lecture	
		11.00	on AIRCRAFT. at 4pm at MOULLE (Refmap STOMER tom. Q.11) Weather	
	5-8-18		overcast with fair intervals. N.C.O despatched to Base (refmap) Weather	
	6-8-18		Downpour. Hostile aircraft shows at EPER LECQUES. (refmap) >7 A.N.E. Serno K.33	C.D
			weather overcast. Training programme attached 1.0.R taken on strength. Weather	with training
	7-8-18	9.15	Training as training programme. Weather good.	programme.
	8-8-18	9.15	Training as training programme. 1 other rank 2/Lt Thorbum engaged in	
			practise for contact aeroplane Weather good.	
	9-8-18	9.15	Training as programme. 1 other rank 2/Lt Thorbum engaged in	
			contact aeroplane exercise ruled by 30th Middlesex Regt. engaged in	
	10-8-18	9.15	Training as programme. Weather good. Stable reverte live. Good aim 10 h.m.	Copy
	11-8-18	8y5	Church Parade. I.B.R. returned from leave weather good	a/43
	12-9-18		Training as programme 2/Lt hands (2/Lt THORNALLEY, 1st SUFFOLK) 7.2. 0742 attached	a/43 programme
			2/Lt NUNN, 1st Middlesex	

WAR DIARY or INTELLIGENCE SUMMARY

Army Form C. 2118.

(Erase heading not required.)

Instructions regarding War Diaries and Intelligence Summaries are contained in F.S. Regs., Part II. and the Staff Manual respectively. Title Pages will be prepared in manuscript.

Place	Date	Hour	Summary of Events and Information	Remarks and references to Appendices
OVEST MONT.	12-8-18		for instruction. Weather very good.	
OVEST MONT.	13-8-18	7.00	Battery left OVEST MONT in reconnaissance with 43rd Inf Bde Orders No 20.	
		10.45	arrived LEDERZEELE (ref map ST OMER 1 G.27. d. H.50.) 10.45	
LEDERZEELE	14-8-18	7.45	G.27. d. H.50. 1.0.72 relieved to rest. 1.0.72 taken over strength	
			Battery left LEDERZEELE (ref map ST OMER 1 G.27.E.99.40) to meet	
			43rd Inf Bde Orders No 28. 43rd Inf Bde Orders No 20.) in accordance with	
BUSSEZEELE		10.50	Arrived BUSSEZEELE HTQ at E.S.O.9.5.	
	15.8.18	7.40	Battery left BUSSEZEELE in reconnaissance (ref map HAZEBROUCK, 5A). Weather good.	
DROGLANDT		12.45	Battery bivouacs in DROGLANDT Orders No 21.	
	16-8-18		1.0.72 taken on strength.	
	17.8.18	7.40	Battery left DROGLANDT K.S.a.S.S. (ref map 5hut 27 Hazebrouck) returned	
PROVEN		10.00	arrived PROVEN (F.7.a.5.5 5hut 27 Proven.). 1.0.72 taken off Bn. Orders No 32.	
			gone to hospital. Weather	
	18.8.18	20	Battery moved by rail into Reserve area in accordance	
			with 43rd Inf Bde S.C. 172.	
A.30. Central		15.15	Arrived A.30 Central (5hut 28)	
YPRES FRONT	19.8.18	21.30	43rd Lh.Bty relieved the 149th Lh Bty on the right Sub sector of Army Battery members	Operation order att'd
			4th Canadian Shelts. (Ref map YPRES town)	
			3/27 Thielman ½ 3/27 THOURNEY took over. Relief complete 00.30 31/8/18	

2449 Wt. W14957/M90 750,000 1/16 J.B.C. & A. Forms/C.2118/12.

Army Form C. 2118.

WAR DIARY
or
INTELLIGENCE SUMMARY
(Erase heading not required.)

Place	Date	Hour	Summary of Events and Information	Remarks and references to Appendices
YPRES FRONT.	August 1918 19	15.30	Position of guns. I.21.6.05.45. I.21.6.05.55. I.21.d.00.03. I.15.d.00.05. I.14.6.30.30. I.14.6.15.30. Battery HQ. (Capt. SRF. HADE, M.C. + 2/Lt Hicks) I.14.6.2.8. LEFT Half Battery O.M. Stone proceeds to RYDE CAMP. (Sheet 28 B.7.a.2.8.) Weather good. Sector quiet. Section in line (not relieved) Bde H.Q. at MACHINE GUN FARM.	A.D.S. CENTRAL
	20	23.00	Morning quiet. Front position's shells in the evening. 2 O.R. wounded. 2 gun position temporarily out of action. Weather good. The two gun position reconstructed. Section ordered. Situation normal.	
	21		Weather good. Situation normal.	
	22 23 24		Situation normal, very quiet. Weather good. 20th Middlesex relieved by 1/5th Suffolk.	
	25	21.30	Left Half Battery under 2/Lt. Davis 7 2/Lt. Nunn relieves Right Half Battery in the line. Reliefs complete by 0.00 56. Weather	
	26	04.30	quiet. Situation normal. Right Half Battery proceeds to RYDE CAMP. (Sheet 28 B.7.a.2.8.)	Thurston Opstr. attd.
	31	22.00	Battery withdrawn from front line to support position in conjunction with Batts in the line (2" Suffolk) to counter the AMERICAN Division	

Army Form C. 2118.

WAR DIARY or INTELLIGENCE SUMMARY

(Erase heading not required.)

Instructions regarding War Diaries and Intelligence Summaries are contained in F.S. Regs., Part II. and the Staff Manual respectively. Title Pages will be prepared in manuscript.

Place	Date	Hour	Summary of Events and Information	Remarks and references to Appendices
YPRES FRONT.	1915 Aug. 27	02.00	On right to carry out a bombing attack. G.O.C. front gave 2 O.C.'s Captain Boynton reoccupied by 3.10.	
	27/28 28		7"/9" By fire returned. L.L.! Weather moderate. Situation normal.	
	29 30.		Weather wet, with two intervals. Situation normally normal. 1. O.R. accidentally wounded. Hostile shelling in afternoon.	18.O.R. (Re-Reserve) Joined RYDE CAMP
	31	04.00 21.30	Regl. Officer [?] Pte Davis. wounded. Weather fair. Regl. Half Battery relieved. 1st Stationary relieved the left half Battery in the line. Relief completed by midnight. Situation Left Half Battery marched to RYDE CAMP.	Officer under No. 3.

43rd Trench Mortar Battery

Training Programme for Week ending August 10th 1918

Day of Week	8.30 - 9.30	9.30 - 10.30	10.45 - 11.45	11.45 - 12.45	2.00 - 3.00
Tuesday	Physical Training and Bayonet fighting	Infantry Training	Gun Drill	Laying & Setting Gun	S.O.S. Class
Wednesday	Physical Training and Bayonet fighting	Musketry and B.F. Drill	Firing Emplacements	Gun Drill	Regimental Games
Thursday	← Musketry Firing, Stripping & application practice (Munition) →		(Practice S.E. 9. C. & 2.)	S.O.S. Class
Friday	← Firing — Stokes Mortar R20 b 21 a 10. 90 11/5 map 27A NE sheet →		Regimental Games	
Saturday	← Firing Stokes Meeting →			Regimental Games

14th Division. *Rfmop. 27ᵗʰ S.E.*

Reference your G.S.338 of 2.8.18; the following exercise will be carried out on August 9th at 10.a.m.

1. **Object of Exercise.**

    (a) To practice the Company in the co-operation and use to the best advantage of all the weapons with which it is armed: with only such artillery support as may be expected in moving warfare.

    (b) The support of Infantry in attacking a defended locality by Light Trench Mortars.

2. **General Idea.**

    The enemy is reported by aircraft to be retiring S.E. and from reliable information received is on the general line NORTBECOURT - INGLINGHEM - HOULE.
    The British hold LA RONVILLE - NORTLEULINGHEM and are following up the enemy.
    Semi-open warfare is in progress.

3. **Special idea.**

    One Company 20th Middlesex Regt (with one section 43rd Trench Mortar Battery) acting as vanguard to the Battalion are pushing forward and on debouching from CULEM locate the enemy holding a strong point on the N.W. side of INGLINGHEM Village. The vanguard Commander decides to attack this strong point and secure the cross roads at INGLINGHEM. (P.24.a.9.6) which has been given him as his objective for the first bound.
    Troops are operating on either flank against NORTBECOURT and Carr de Marne and 20th Middlesex Regt. is in touch with them.

4. **Details.**

    Blank ammunition for rifles will be issued at the rate of 15 rounds per man: rattles will be used to represent Lewis Guns.
    Live Stokes Mortar ammunition and Rifle Grenades will be used.
    The enemy will be represented by Targets or Dummies.

5. Officer Commanding the attacking force will have his local protection in position, with remainder of Company in N.W. of CULEM, at 10.a.m. when the operations commence.

6. O.C. 20th Middlesex Regt. will post sentries to block roads and warn inhabitants.

7. O.C. 20th Middlesex Regt. will detail one Company for the exercise.

8. O.C. 43rd Light Trench Mortar Battery will detail one section of guns which, together with the ammunition, will be carried on pack animals, to be borrowed from the 20th Middlesex Regt.

9. **Dress.** Fighting order.

10. No digging will be done.

T. P. Coe
Captain,
Brigade Major,
43rd Infantry Brigade.

6.8.18.

Copies to:-
20th Middx Regt.
43rd T.M. Battery.

SECRET.   Copy No 7

43rd Trench Mortar Battery Operation Orders No 1.

Reference Map Sheet 28 1/20000 & YPRES 1/10000   August 18th 1918

1. The 43rd T.M. Bty will relieve the 148th T.M. Bty in the Right Sub-sector of the 49th Divisional Sector on the night of August 19-20. 1918.

2. The 148th T.M. Bty is providing guides who will be at Machine Gun Farm Siding at 11.30 p.m.

3. Gun positions, Range Cards, Ammunition Dumps, Programmes of work, Defence schemes, Secret Maps and Trench Stores will be taken over and list forwarded to Battery H.Qrs.

4. 2/Lt. Hicks will take over Trench Stores by daylight August 19th 1918.

5. Completion of relief will be reported to Battery H.Qrs by runner by the code word EXCELLENT.

6. Battery H.Qrs. will be at I.14.b.2.8

7. 148th T.M. Bty is arranging for one Officer to remain in the line for 24 hours after relief.

8. Acknowledge.

Issued at 10 p.m.

Copies to.
1. O.C
2. 2nd in Command
3. 2/Lt Harbison
4. B. of M.S
5. O/C 148th T.M. Bty (for information)
6. 43rd Inf. Bde. (for information)
7. War Diary.

                                  [signature] Capt
                        Comdg. 43rd T.M. Bty

SECRET   COPY N°... 6

43rd Trench Mortar Battery
Operation Order N° 2.

Reference: map YPRES 1/10000 and 28 1/40000

23/8/18.

1. The left half Battery will relieve the right half Battery in the line on the night of August 25/26.

2. Guides will be at Battery H.Q @ 9 p.m.

3. Gun positions, Range cards, Ammunition, Defence schemes and Trench Stores will be handed over.

4. On relief, right half Battery, will move to Detail Camp at G 4 a 1.9 Sheet 28.

5. Completion of relief will be reported to Battery H.Q by Officer i/c right half Battery, and thence to Brigade H.Q by code word "BUTTER"

6. Acknowledge.

Issued at 10 p.m

Copies to:-
1. O.C.
2. Officer i/c Right half Battery
3.   "   "   Left   "   "
4. 43rd Infantry Brigade (for information)
5. 12th Suffolks.
6. War Diary ✓

A. Rowland Steele
Captain
Commanding 43rd T.M.B.ty.

SECRET.   COPY No. 5

43rd Trench Mortar Battery
OPERATION ORDER No. 3.

Reference Map Sheet 28.   30th August 1918.

1. The Right Half Battery will relieve the Left Half Battery in the Right Sub-Sector of 14th Divisional Front. night of 31/1st Sept.

2. Guides will be at Battery H.Qs at 9 p.m.

3. Gun Positions, Range Cards, Ammunition, Defence Schemes, Trench Stores &c., will be handed over.

4. On Relief, Left Half Battery will move to Ryde Camp, 28t 4a, 2.8.

5. Completion of relief will be reported to Battery H.Qs by Officer i/c Left Half Battery, and then to Brigade H.Qs by code word "SUGAR"

6. Acknowledge.

COPIES TO:-

1. OC
2. Officer i/c Right Half Battery.
3. " " Left " "
4. 43rd Infantry Brigade
5. War Diary.

_____
Captain
Commanding 43rd T.M.Bty.

SECRET.

45th French Mortar Battery, [illegible]

[illegible date]

1. The Left half Battery will relieve the Right Battery in the [illegible]

2. [illegible] Range [illegible] [illegible] will be handed over.

3. Guides will be at Battery H.Q. [illegible]

4. Completion of relief will be reported to Battery H.Q. by O.C. Right half Battery and then to Brigade H.Q. by the [illegible] SODA

5. [illegible] Right half Battery [illegible]
   [illegible]

6. Acknowledge.

Issued at 11.00 a.m.

Copies to:—
1. C.O.
2. O.C. Left half Battery
3. O.C. Right half Battery
4. [illegible] Infantry Brigade
5. [illegible] Suffolks
6. D.T.O.
7. War Diary

[signature] Aide
Capt.
[illegible], 45th [illegible]

WAR DIARY or INTELLIGENCE SUMMARY

Army Form C. 2118.

43 T M Bty

Place	Date	Hour	Summary of Events and Information	Remarks and references to Appendices
YPRES FRONT. MAP (28 NWE)	1-9-18		Situation normal. Weather fair.	
	2-9-18	23.00	10" H.L.1 relieved by 9th Middlesex. Situation quiet. Weather fair.	
	3-9-18		Quiet early morning. Slight enemy shelling of W. bank of ZILLEBEKE LAKE. Afternoon situation quiet. Weather good.	
	4-9-18		Situation normal with slight enemy shelling of W. bank of ZILLEBEKE. Weather warm.	
	5.		Situation quiet. Weather warm.	
	6.		Situation normal. Weather fine. 2 or 3 returns from hospital.	
	20th HE		relieved by 15th Suffolks.	
	7.	21.30	LEFT. HALF Battery relieved 2/LT NUNN relieving RIGHT. HALF Battery in the line. Relief completed by 11.30 pm. Situation quiet. Heavy thunderstorm. RIGHT HALF Battery moved to RYDE CAMP. 2/LT THORNLEY remained at B Battery H.Q.	
	8.	4.10	2/Lt Hicks to line. LEFT HALF Battery in the line. Situation normal.	
	9.		Situation normal. Weather warmer.	
	10		Situation normal. Weather warm. 2/Lt Bolham Dawson. took over position B line. B.O by Relay of B Company of the 12th	
	4/11		Suffolks.	
	11.	21.30	Situation quiet. Weather unsettled. Forward position dug at I.24.c.70.95 infront 28 NW Sheet	

2449 Wt. W14957/M90 750,000 1/16 J.B.C. & A. Forms/C.2118/12.

WAR DIARY or INTELLIGENCE SUMMARY

Army Form C. 2118.

Place	Date	Hour	Summary of Events and Information	Remarks and references to Appendices
YPRES FRONT.	11.	21.30	To front on Mag. bearing 130°. Supports relieved by 10th H.L.I.	
	12.	21.45	Situation quiet. Weather mild. RIGHT HALF BATTERY under 2/Lt. HARBISON relieves LEFT HALF Battery in the line. Relief completed by 23.30. LEFT HALF Battery moved to RYDE CAMP. Situation normal. Weather improved. Guns at I.11.d.05.55.7. I.15.d.00.03. withdrawn (B.M. 173)	
	13.	20.30	43rd Bde relieves in the line. RIGHT HALF Battery withdrawn in accordance with 43rd Bde order No.32. Battery MQ closes at I.14.b.2.9 at 20.30. LEFT HALF Battery proceeds to SCHOOL CAMP (Sheet 7.L3C.7.) by march route. RIGHT HALF Battery after withdrawing from the	
	14.	22.00	the line entrains at GOODERICH SIDING. (Sheet 28. I.C.11.8) Arrives SCHOOL CAMP. Battery moves BLUE GRASS arriving (Sheet 27 F.28.C.19.)	
SCHOOL CAMP Ref.map.27. L.3.C.55.	15.	1.30 1.45	RIGHT HALF Battery. Weather mild in morning. Heavy rain later. 2 O.R. returns from Hospital. 30.R. reports sick.	
	16.		Weather fine. 2 O.R. returns from Hospital.	
	17.		Rest Camp. Training (Physical Training, Infantry Training, Gun Drill, Musketry) weather good.	
	18.		Training (Physical Training, Infantry Training, Gun Drill) Weather good.	
	19.		Training (Physical Training, Infantry Training, Gun Drill, Musketry) average.	

WAR DIARY or INTELLIGENCE SUMMARY

Army Form C. 2118.

Place	Date	Hour	Summary of Events and Information	Remarks and references to Appendices
SCHOOL Camp D. (57/c.3.c.55)	19.		Weather good.	
	20.	19.00	2/Lieut J.C.A. Kincaid Smith 10th H.L.I. & 2.0.T.C. taken on strength. 1/3rd The Battery moves to DOMINION CAMP returning (Philip) 23. C.8.6. in accordance with H.Q. 1st Inf Bde order No. 33. 4.35 Inf Bde orders H.Q. 4.2 Inf Bde in the left sub section of the 1st Divisional Front from I.32.d.25.35 to I.33.c.0.9.	Orders attached
DOMINION CAMP Sheet 28. C.22.C.8.6.	21.	23.30	Battery arrived DOMINION CAMP. Weather good. O.C. (Capt. S.R.F. Hyde M.C.) & 2/Lt Hicks reconnoitre line. No scope for L.T.M.S. Weather good.	
	22		Battery at DOMINION CAMP. Weather good.	
	23		Weather good.	
C.28.b.SP.99	24	13.30	Battery moves to B.U. TRANSPORT LINES at C.21.B.20.99. Weather good.	
	25		Weather good.	
	26		Weather good.	
	27	18.30	Left Battery under 2/Lt Harbison and 2/Lt Thornbury and went in advance with H.Q. 3rd Inf Bde under No 37 H.Q. 3rd Inf Bde orders. G.S. 630. (Strength 2 officers & 60 O.R.) Battery H.Q. (Capt S.R.F. Hyde M.C. 30 R2) moves to Advanced Bde H.Q. at H.sr.c. 50.ss.	
LINE. Ref. maps 28 N.W.4 29 S.W.2	28.	23.00 4.15	Any Battery arrived at Lankof Chan. H.32.a 90.96 (ref. map 28 N.W.4) 4/4 man in aeroplane with H.3rd Bde overlooking enemy lines with 4/5 rounds various from H.32.a 90.96 to roughly forward 1.33.a.	

2449 Wt. W14957/M90 750,000 1/16 J.B.C. & A. Forms/C.2118/12.

WAR DIARY or INTELLIGENCE SUMMARY

Army Form C. 2118.

Place	Date	Hour	Summary of Events and Information	Remarks and references to Appendices
Pl. not. 19. 28 N.W.4 28 S.W.2	19.	4-4am	2nd and 3rd lines formed up behind support platoon 1 Coy 1st Suffolks facing MIDDLESEX ROAD & North of CANAL.	
		5.30.	ZERO HOUR. Battery moved forwards in rear of 1st Suffolks and continued to move along N. of CANAL, & other 3 detachments moved along S. bank as far as I.33.d.30.60. From there No. 2 detachment moved along Inside bank of CANAL. Nos. 3 & 4 followed railway running from I.33.d. to 30 (O.3.90.80. No. 1 detachment on N. side of CANAL were detained by W. STAFF on left & crossed on through RAVINE WOOD. I.34.c. Established gun positions at I.34.c. 60.60 to form a reverse Ludenhof network of Battery at O.3.90.80. No. 2 detachment worked along inwards & CANAL BANK from at I.33.d.90.20 came under enemy fire from M.G. Build on T.O.P. RIDGE, losing One Officer (2/Lt. HARRISON) 2/Lt. THRONALLY assumed command. No 3 detachment after following railway as far as O.2.10.70	

2449 Wt. W14957/M90 750,000 1/16 J.B.C. & A. Forms/C.2118/12.

WAR DIARY or INTELLIGENCE SUMMARY

Army Form C. 2118.

Place	Date	Hour	Summary of Events and Information	Remarks and references to Appendices
LINE in front of 69.N.14. & 28.S.W.2.	28.	6.30.	Were unable to move further owing to enemy machine gun fire. Headquarters were withdrawn up to Coy 1st Suffolks Battalion H.Qrs. at I.33.d.70.00. Stanton reports (6) Battery H.Qrs. at 9.00 a.m. This member of the Battery was extremely good work (at Pr.O.). who being cut off from his took charge of the gun (Corpl Morgan was wounded) & in spite of N. Staffs retaining 3/4 manning No. 23095 Pte MERRIMAN, who knowing details from his gun team threw the shells he was carrying at enemy in an war party established attempting to bring back his officer who had been hit. The fog having closed his officer redeemed in one of counter attacks. No.300289 Pte CLAXTON who saved his life.	Note 303 (see Pr.O.)
G.31.6.90.99 (in front of Belgian Lines)	29.	19.00	H.3" Brigade with brown from line, accordingly H.3" J.R.B. moved to G.31.6.90.99. via YPRES-MEZEELE-DICKEBUSCH-OUDERDOM-BUSSEBOOM. arriving 22.15. The march of the men during the night was splendid, no stragglers. Total casualties 1 officer (S/Lt HARBISON) killed & 10 OR killed, wounded during operations which end June
	30.		Cleaning guns the reorganizing.	

2449 Wt. W14957/M90 750,000 1/16 J.B.C. & A. Forms/C.2118/12.

SECRET.   Copy No. 1.

Operation Order No. 6.

Reference Maps: Sheet 28 N.W. 1/20,000 & Sheet 27 1/40,000

September 14th 1918

1. On the night of 14/15th - 43rd Brigade is being relieved - RIGHT HALF BATTERY will withdraw from line to SCHOOL CAMP 27/L.3.c.5.5. in accordance with 43rd Infantry Bde Order. No 32.

2. RIGHT HALF BATTERY will entrain at 10 p.m. at GODERICH SIDING. Sheet 28/I.1.c.1.8. and detrain at BLUE GRASS Sheet 27/F.28.c.1.9.

3. Trench Stores, ammunition, defence schemes etc will be handed over to 1/1 Yorkshire Dragoons.

4. Billeting Party to be detailed by Officer i/c Details will report to Area Commandant HIPSHOEK. at 27/L.3.c.7.7.

5. One Lorry will report to Q.M. Stores at 10 a.m.

6. Details will proceed to SCHOOL CAMP by March Route.

7. Guides to be detailed by Officer i/c Details will be at detraining point to guide Right-half Battery to Camp.

8. Battery. H. Qrs will close at I.14.b.2.8 at 8.30 p.m. 14th and re-open at SCHOOL CAMP on arrival.

9. Acknowledge.

Issued at 10.00 a.m.

Rowla Hide Capt.

14. 9. 18.   Commanding. 43rd Trench Mortar Bty.

SECRET.   Copy. No. 7

43rd Trench Mortar Battery
Operation Order No 5

Reference Map. YPRES 1/10000. 28 1/40000

11th September 1917

1. The RIGHT. HALF Battery will relieve the LEFT. HALF Battery in the line on the night of Sept. 12/13th.

2. Guides will be at Battery H.Q. at 7.p.m.

3. Gun positions, Range cards, Trench Stores and work on hand will be handed over.

4. On relief, LEFT. HALF Battery will move to RYDE CAMP.

5. Completion of relief will be reported to Battery H.Q. by O/c LEFT HALF Bty and thence to Brigade H.Q. by code word. "FUEL".

6. Acknowledge.

Issued at 2.30 p.m.

G. Rowland Hill
Captain
Commanding. 43rd T.M. Bty.

Copies to:-
1. O.C.
2. Officer i/c RIGHT. HALF Bty
3. " i/c LEFT "
4. 43rd Infantry Bde.
5. 1/ York & Lancs
6. 10th H.L.I.
7 WAR. DIARY ✓

"O" FORM.
MESSAGES AND SIGNALS.

Army Form C. 2123.
(In books of 100.)
No. of Message......

Prefix........Code......Words..........	Received.	Sent, or sent out.	Office Stamp.
£ s. d.	From............	At..............m.	
Charges to Collect	By............		
Service Instructions		To..............	
FF7		By............	

Handed in at......B.A.F..........Office 5.47.m. Received 6.7.m.

TO ...... PAVO

*Sender's Number.	Day of Month.	In reply to Number.	AAA

Will ... ... right
guns tonight to
Transport lines ...
This cancels from self
my order 21 which I
will send you shortly
aaa Addressed
PAVO repeated WABO aaa
from PAVO acknowledge

FROM PLACE & TIME ...... FF7 ......

*This line should be erased if not required.

noms
ask noms for his
report aplease

9.50p.
9.5up.

9.40p — A768 Bosu Loku
9.5up   C61. PC   Ey13

7

43rd Trench Mortar Battery
Move Order

September 20th, 1918.

Reference Map. 28 1/20,000

1. On the night of the 20th - 43rd T. M. Bty will move to DOMINION CAMP G.23.b.8.6 in accordance with 43rd Inf Bde Order No 33.

2. Dress - Marching Order.

3. Advance party will proceed to DOMINION CAMP at 10 a.m.

4. One Lorry will report to Q.M. Stores at 7.45 a.m. and will be used for two journeys.

5. Q.M. Stores to be ready by 9.30 a.m.

6. Officers Kits, Orderly Room, & Canteen Stores & Cooks Utensils to be ready at 5.30 p.m.

B. Rowland Hide, Capt.
Comdg 43rd T. M. Bty.